EXTREME WEATHER AHEAD!

EDITED BY JOANNE RANDOLPH

SUNDAY MONDAY TUESDAY WEDNESDAY THURSDAY FRIDAY SATURDAY

This edition published in 2018 by:
Enslow Publishing, LLC.
101 W. 23rd Street, Suite 240
New York, NY 10011

Additional materials copyright © 2018 by Enslow Publishing, LLC

Cataloging-in-Publication Data

Names: Randolph, Joanne, editor.
Title: Extreme weather ahead! / edited by Joanne Randolph.
Description: New York : Enslow Publishing, 2018 | Series: The weather report |
Includes bibliographical references and index. | Audience: Grades 3-5.
Identifiers: ISBN 9780766090118 (library bound) | ISBN 9780766090095 (pbk.) | ISBN 9780766090101 (6 pack)
Subjects: LCSH: Climatic extremes--Juvenile literature. | Storms--Juvenile literature. | Weather--Juvenile literature.
Classification: LCC QC981.8.C53 E94 2018 | DDC 551.55--dc23
Printed in the United States of America

To Our Readers: We have done our best to make sure all website addresses in this book were active and appropriate when we went to press. However, the author and the publisher have no control over and assume no liability for the material available on those websites or on any websites they may link to. Any comments or suggestions can be sent by e-mail to customerservice@enslow.com.

Photos Credits: Cover, p. 1 eddtoro / Shutterstock.com (blizzard), solarseven/Shutterstock.com (weather symbols); series logo, NPeter/Shutterstock.com; interior pages background image, back cover, Sabphoto/Shutterstock.com; pp. 3, 28, 30, 32 Igor Zh./Shutterstock.com; pp. 4, 8, 14, 19 Greg Lundeen/www.srh.noaa.gov; p. 5 NOAA/Getty Images; p. 6 Joe Raedle/Getty Images; p. 7 inhauscreative/E+/Getty Images; p. 9 Mark Burnett/Alamy Stock Photo; p. 10 Science Source; p. 12 Alain Jocard/AFP/Getty Images; p. 15 zhuyongming/Moment/Getty Images; p. 16 Scott Olson/Getty Images; p. 17 AFP/Getty Images; p. 21 Topical Press Agency/Hulton Archive/Getty Images; p. 22 Corbis/Getty Images; p. 23 Library of Congress/Corbis/Getty Images; p. 26 Heritage Images/Hulton Fine Art Collection/Getty Images.

Article Credits: Kathiann M. Kowalski, "Extreme Weather," *Odyssey*; Stephen James O'Meara, "Nature's Fury: For Better or Worse," *Odyssey*.

CONTENTS

A GLIMPSE OF THINGS TO COME?

When Hurricane Matthew hammered the Caribbean islands and the southeast coast in October 2016, it toppled trees and houses, knocked out power, and caused much coastal flooding. It was a Category 4 hurricane on the Saffir-Simpson Wind Scale, which measures the strength of a hurricane from 1 (weakest) to 5 (strongest) based on its wind speed. A few months earlier, massive flooding devastated Louisiana, causing major damage to some 146,000 homes and leaving hundreds of thousands of people homeless. A few days later, an outbreak of tornadoes scoured the countryside in Ohio and Indiana. What made this outbreak notable for the area was that it happened in August (a slow month for tornadoes) and it caught **meteorologists** off-guard. Meanwhile, several areas of the country were experiencing extreme to moderate drought conditions, which sorely **impacted** agriculture and water supplies in the affected areas.

Get ready for more battering by bad weather. Although it's impossible to blame **global warming** for specific events in 2016, convincing **predictions** say that both floods and droughts will become more common, and perhaps more extreme, worldwide.

Hurricanes, heat waves, floods, droughts, and tornadoes have all happened before. And over millions of years, Earth's **climate** has naturally gone from warm periods to ice ages and back again. When scientists talk

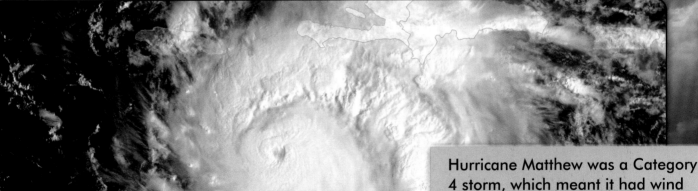

Hurricane Matthew was a Category 4 storm, which meant it had wind speeds of 130 to156 miles (209 to 251 kilometers) per hour.

5

about global warming or global climate change, however, they're focusing on possible human impacts since the **Industrial Revolution**. Every day, factories, power plants, motor vehicles, and other sources emit tons of carbon dioxide and other "greenhouse gases." Basically, greenhouse gases trap extra heat in Earth's **atmosphere**, warming it slightly above what it would have been otherwise.

Since 1988, the Intergovernmental Panel on Climate Control (IPCC) has been studying greenhouse gases' potential impacts. In 2007, the group's Fourth Assessment Report said it was "very likely" that

The flooded streets of Port Vincent, Louisiana, were caused by torrential rains.

Factories can send lots of pollution into the atmosphere.

greenhouse gas **emissions** from human activities caused most of Earth's average temperature increase for the preceding sixty years. By 2100, the IPCC estimates, average global temperatures will climb between 2 degrees and 11.5 degrees Fahrenheit (1.1 degrees to 6.4 degrees Celsius). Normally, we won't feel differences of just a couple of degrees. The real problem is the possibility for more very hot days and other extreme events. "In climate **models** what you see is that when you add more greenhouse gases to the atmosphere, the extremes change more than the averages do," says Jay Gulledge at the Pew Center on Global Climate Change. "It's the extreme weather events that cause damage, not the average."

CHAPTER TWO

WAS CLIMATE CHANGE THE CULPRIT?

Which of 2016's bad weather events came about because of climate change? Scientists can't really say. "You cannot attribute any single day's event to global warming," says Tom Peterson at the National Climatic Data Center in North Carolina.

"The atmosphere is what scientists call a **chaotic** system," explains Gulledge. "It follows the laws of **physics**, of course. But with very, very small disturbances of the atmosphere, many, many, many different things can possibly happen." Thus, you can't work backwards from one specific result to one particular cause.

A meteorologist studies a weather map. Meteorologists track weather and long-term climate trends, among many other jobs.

NATURAL FORCES

Beyond this, natural forces play major roles in causing weather. In the past as with today, extreme weather, such as Texas's hot, dry summer of 2011 was driven largely by **La Niña**, a weather pattern linked to cooler waters in the Pacific Ocean. A warming and cooling cycle in the

variable
Polar Jet Stream

colder

H
blocking
high pressure

wetter

wetter

warmer

drier

drier

This image shows a La Niña winter and how it affects the weather in North America. You can see the areas that are warmer, wetter, or drier than they would be under normal winter weather patterns.

Atlantic, called the Atlantic Multidecadal Oscillation, also played a part. Drier ground made temperatures even hotter.

"We probably would have broken the record [for high temperatures] even without the global temperature increase," notes Texas State Climatologist John Nielsen-Gammon. And it's hard to tell whether global warming will increase or decrease Texas rainfall in the long run, he says.

One extra degree can make a drought more widespread and severe. More importantly, the climate is still adjusting to greenhouse gas emissions, which keep going up. "The relative importance of climate change is just going to keep increasing over time," says Nielsen-Gammon.

TRYING TO MAKE SENSE OF THE DATA

So far, several studies have used **forecasting** models to try to link climate change to specific events. In one study of conditions like those before Great Britain's floods in 2000, two-thirds of the model runs had greater flood risks with greenhouse gas emissions than without them. Another study concluded that greenhouse gas emissions doubled the chances of Europe's 2003 heat wave from about one thousand to one to five hundred to one. Both cases gave odds that global warming had an impact—not a definitive yes or no.

Climate change has become a global issue. Here people are discussing the price of carbon in a 2015 conference on climate change in Le Bourget, France.

Rather than focusing on individual weather events, suggests Gulledge, ask how likely they are to happen in the future. "If they used to happen once every ten years, and they now happen once every four years, that change is statistical," he says. "And that we can attribute to warming."

Gulledge and Jeff Masters at the website Weather Underground both use the concept of dice to think about risks of extreme weather from climate change. Suppose that instead of rolling a number from two to twelve, one of the dice has seven faces, so you can now roll from two to thirteen. Suppose also that the dice are loaded, so larger numbers come up more often.

In a similar way, climate change may expand the range of what extreme weather events can happen. It will also make extreme events more likely.

CHAPTER THREE

WHAT CAN WE EXPECT?

"Increases in extremes in heat are one area where we will first see the effects of global warming," says Masters. Very hot days are likely to become more common, and new records might be set.

Heavy precipitation is also likely to increase in many areas. A warmer atmosphere causes more evaporation. "If you have more water vapor in the air," says Masters, "that means more of it can come down as rain in heavy rainfall events."

In **arid** areas, however, higher extreme temperatures increase chances for drought and wildfires. Warmer air evaporates more water, drying the ground. "The temperatures get hotter as the ground gets drier," adds Nielsen-Gammon. "The additional extreme temperatures make wildfires

Long-term drought is a problem in many areas. Land that doesn't get water over time becomes cracked and drained of nutrients.

much more likely, and those fires that do form become larger and affect more land."

On the flip side, climate change will probably mean fewer bitterly cold days. But fewer record cold days could also mean more snowstorms. "The heaviest snowfalls always occur right around freezing," explains Masters. "That's when the atmosphere is still cold enough to snow, but you have the maximum amount of water vapor in the air."

Will hurricanes become more common? That question is still "up in the air," says Gulledge. "The indications at this point are that on a global basis, total hurricanes are likely to become less frequent, but the strongest ones [will become] more frequent." Research is ongoing.

Likewise, it's tough to tell whether climate change will bring more or fewer tornadoes. "Major tornado outbreaks require a whole bunch

15

Precipitation, including record snowfalls, could increase with global warming.

of things to come together," notes Peterson. Those factors include **wind shear**, thunderstorm clouds, and other conditions. "You can't really say that that's going to be more common in the future or not, based upon the information," says Peterson.

LOOKING AHEAD

Climate models and weather forecasts both look toward the future, but they're two different things. "Climate is what you expect. Weather is what you get," says Masters, quoting from American author Mark Twain.

Because the atmosphere is chaotic, weather forecasting works up to about one week ahead. In contrast, climate models calculate average conditions several decades or a hundred years in the future.

"The biggest unmet need is that people want five- to ten-year forecasts," says Peterson. Providing that information is tough, though, because science can't yet pinpoint when events like **El Niño** and La Niña will happen.

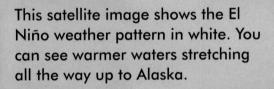

10 NOV 97

JPL

NASA cnes

This satellite image shows the El Niño weather pattern in white. You can see warmer waters stretching all the way up to Alaska.

Nonetheless, communities need to make decisions. Cities and towns might expand systems for handling storm water if increased flood risks justified the cost. Or, if science could say when droughts were likely, farmers could adjust crops and herd sizes and invest in better water conservation.

Some efforts seek to build regional weather forecasting into part of a longer-term climate model. Other researchers are refining the data used in climate models. For example, some now start with current ocean conditions instead of historical averages.

Meanwhile, as we cope with what's happening now, today's extreme weather can also help us prepare for tomorrow's risks. "That identifies places where we need to take adaptation measures," says Gulledge. "It also helps put a dollar value and a human cost value on the consequences of climate change."

Is Global Warming Real?

While some skeptics argue to the contrary, most climate scientists agree that human activities are indeed causing climate change. A 2010 study published by the National Academies of Science found that 97 percent of climate scientists agree with the IPCC that the **evidence** is sufficient to show that human activities have caused most of Earth's increased average temperatures over the last sixty years.

NATURE'S FURY

Hurricanes, tornadoes, droughts, floods, blizzards, cold snaps, monsoons, typhoons, and more happen each and every year. Severe weather affects millions of people—and even takes lives—across the globe every day. And it seems to be getting worse.

It might seem as if severe weather around the globe is on the rise, in part, because of improvements in communication and technology. Thirty years ago, we did not have the internet or cable news. A hundred years ago there were no radios, no TV. 'Round-the-clock coverage of the weather was what you observed around you.

Today we hear more about severe weather because there are more people and ways to report it … immediately! Weather satellites circle the globe, constantly monitoring Earth. When a tornado touches down in Kansas, a hurricane approaches Florida, or a flood washes away homes in Egypt, we hear about it and see pictures within hours.

And though scientists are studying the impact of human-caused climate change, and they think they see a correlation in the increase of extreme events, the fact is, severe weather—even dramatic climate change —has always been a part of Earth's history. Indeed, some of the storms we have experienced in recent years pale in comparison to those that occurred early in the twentieth century and before. Let's look back in time to a few of the many remarkable weather events in modern history.

THE GREAT TRI-STATE TORNADO OF 1925

On March 18, 1925, the most devastating and powerful tornado in American history touched down near Ellington, Missouri. The hideous funnel cloud was about a quarter-mile (½ km) in width but at times grew as wide as a mile (about 1 ½ km).

Shortly after touching down, the twister crossed the Mississippi River about 75 miles (121 km) southeast of St. Louis. It then traveled 219 miles (352 ½ km) on the ground, plowing through southern Illinois and southwestern Indiana at 60 miles (96 ½ km) per hour. It completely ripped apart four towns and severely damaged six. It destroyed fifteen thousand

Griffin, Indiana, was devastated in the tri-state tornado that struck the area in 1925.

homes, some of which were lifted into the air—where they exploded like bombs. Before dissipating, the tornado had injured two thousand people and killed 695—a record for a single tornado. Now called the Great Tri-State Tornado, the storm left behind ghost towns, solemn graves, and stories of horror that are passed on from generation to generation.

BLACK SUNDAY (APRIL 14, 1935)

The story of Black Sunday began in 1931, when a severe drought hit the Great Plains of the United States. As crops died and farmlands dried, dust began to blow. The following year, fourteen dust storms struck the region; that number doubled in 1933 (locals counted 139 "dirty days" that year).

Then, on May 11, 1934, a major dust storm brewed in the Dakotas; airborne particles sailed clear across the states to the eastern seaboard. Dense sand blotted out the sun over Washington, DC, 2,000 miles (3,219 km) away. The storm also drove grit between the teeth of New Yorkers and dusted the decks of ships 300 miles (483 km) out to sea! Meanwhile, heat records soared in the Great Plains; record highs were broken on a regular basis. Hundreds of people died in the heat.

During the 1930s, dust storms were common in areas where drought had ravaged vegetation, leaving soil unprotected from winds.

Nearly a year later, the bleak scene repeated itself. This time, the dust blew in from the drying farmlands of Kansas, Colorado, Texas, and Oklahoma. One headline screamed, "The Worst Dust Storm in History." Some two million acres of farmland were evacuated overnight. Children in the Midwest scurried to school with moistened cloths clutched to their noses. So much sand fell in Kansas that an oil driller reported digging down 18 feet (5 ½ meters) and finding nothing but dry powder all the way. But the worst was yet to come.

On Sunday, April 14, 1935, after weeks of devastating dust storms, huge black clouds suddenly appeared on the horizon across the Plains. In no time, people were under a "black blizzard"—as dust clouds more than 1,000 feet (305 m) high and many miles wide swept through the Great Plains at a rate of 60 miles (96 ½ km) per hour.

23

During these stormy years, hundreds of thousands of families left the Plains, abandoning their homes and fields. Millions of acres of farmland had become useless. Still the dust continued to blow—but at less intense levels—until 1939!

1816: The "Year Without a Summer"

As with many major weather phenomena, a series of smaller events can lead up to a big one. In this case, the catalyst was three major volcanic eruptions that took place between 1812 and 1817: Soufrière on St. Vincent Island in the Caribbean erupted in 1812; Mayon in the Philippines erupted in 1814; and Mt. Tambora in what is now Indonesia erupted in 1815.

Together, these volcanoes ejected billions of cubic yards of fine volcanic dust high into the atmosphere. Such dust partially shields Earth from the sun's rays, but permits heat to escape from it. The result is lowered temperatures. In the **annals** of weather, the year 1816 is called "the year without a summer" or the year "eighteen hundred froze to death."

In brief, in 1816 people throughout the northeastern United States, Canada, and parts of Europe experienced a series of totally unexpected cold spells. These occurred continuously through late spring, summer, and early fall. Heavy snow fell in the United States in June and frost formed even in July and August! Farmers' crops were repeatedly killed by the cold.

In northern Vermont, snow drifted 18 to 20 inches (46 to 51 centimeters) deep in June. Ice formed an inch (2 ½ cm) thick on standing water and icicles reached a foot (30 ½ cm) long! Thousands of birds froze to death.

1645: The Little Ice Age

Actually, 1816 was just one of a series of exceptionally cold years. Beginning in 1812, it was cold over the whole world. In fact, some scientists argue that "The Year Without a Summer" was at the tail end of a Little Ice Age.

The cold streak may have begun as early as the 1200s, although many scientists believe it started around the year 1450. Alan Cutler, a visiting scientist at the National Museum of Natural History, says the Little Ice Age was not a single cold snap but a long and complex event. "The cooling trend began at different times in different parts of the world," he says, "and often was interrupted by periods of relative warmth."

The year 1645, however, is cited in many reference books as the high point of the Age. That's when, throughout the world, from Norway to New Zealand, glaciers in mountainous areas were rapidly advancing. In the European Alps, for instance, people watched as some glaciers slowly engulfed farms and crushed entire villages. Across the globe, temperatures plunged to record lows. Much of the North Atlantic was choked with ice; Inuit, Cutler says, had to paddle their kayaks as far south as Scotland to fish! Severe winters in the Jiang-Xi province of China killed the last of the orange groves that had thrived there for centuries.

The effects of the Little Ice Age rippled through Europe for more than five centuries. In his book, *The Little Ice Age,* University of California archaeology professor Brian Fagan argues that the Little Ice Age announced its arrival with the Great Famine of 1315–1321, which in turn may have set the stage for the Hundred Years War. The social and political effects of the Little Ice Age may also have led to the Great Irish Potato Famine, which caused so many of the Irish to migrate to the United States.

Dutch artist Abraham Hondius painted this scene of people skating on the River Thames in London in 1677, when the effects of the Little Ice Age were still being felt.

Since most of the Little Ice Age occurred well before the Industrial Revolution and the widespread burning of fossil fuels, these factors could not have caused it. The event was most likely the result of one or more natural causes—such as a violent and prolonged episode of volcanic activity or a lull in solar activity, or both. Whatever the cause, scientists agree that the Little Ice Age lasted for centuries, and that the world began emerging from its grip between 1850 and 1900.

The 150-year-long (and running) warming trend that we are now experiencing just might be Earth's way of "warming its toes" after spending a long time in the cold.

And in the End. . .

So when you read about global warming and the havoc it might cause, it is good to think about ways we can help our environment, but it is also important to remember that Earth's climate has shifted repeatedly and dramatically over time, even ones as short as a decade—and that it is likely to do so in the future. Be mindful of how you treat our planet so extreme weather doesn't increase in frequency, but remember that … weather happens!

GLOSSARY

annals Historical records.

arid Dry.

atmosphere The blanket of air surrounding a planet.

chaotic Without order or rules.

climate The specific weather conditions in a particular area.

El Niño A climate event that results from warmer-than-usual waters in the tropical Pacific Ocean

emissions The products released from something, especially a gas or radiation.

evidence The facts supporting whether or not something is true; proof.

forecasting Using historic data to predict future trends.

global warming A gradual increase in the overall temperature of Earth's atmosphere due to the greenhouse effect caused by increased levels of carbon dioxide and other pollutants in the atmosphere.

impact To affect something.

Industrial Revolution The period from 1760 to 1850, when manufacturing went through a major shift from manual labor to machines.

La Niña A climate event that results from cooler-than-usual waters in the tropical Pacific Ocean.

meteorologist A person who studies the weather and makes predictions on future weather after analyzing weather data.

model A representation of an object, idea, or process that helps one study and better understand that object, idea, or process. A model can be used to make predictions.

physics The branch of science that focuses on the nature and properties of matter and energy.

prediction A guess or forecast based on information and past experience about future events.

wind shear A high-altitude shift in wind speed or direction.

FURTHER READING

Books

Editors of Kingfisher. *Wild Weather*. New York, NY: Kingfisher, 2016.

Kostigen, Thomas M. *Extreme Weather: Surviving Tornadoes, Sandstorms, Hailstorms, Blizzards, Hurricanes, and More!* Washington, DC: National Geographic Kids, 2015.

Roker, Al. *Al Roker's Extreme Weather*. New York, NY: HarperCollins, 2017.

Squire, Ann. *Extreme Weather*. New York, NY: Scholastic, 2014.

WEBSITES

NASA's Climate Kids
climatekids.nasa.gov/menu/weather-and-climate/
Learn more about climate change and play a climate trivia game.

Weather for Kids
www.sciencekids.co.nz/weather.html
Read weather facts, perform experiments, view images, play games, watch videos, and more.

Weather Wiz Kids
www.weatherwizkids.com/#
Dive deeper into different types of extreme weather.

INDEX